Dear Anaïs

My Life in Poems for You

Diana M. Raab

Plain View Press
P. O. 42255
Austin, TX 78704

plainviewpress.net
sb@plainviewpress.net
1-512-441-2452

Cover design by Amy C. King.

Contents

Preface

Why would poet Diana Raab choose diarist Anaïs Nin as audience for her precisely crafted poems, when she never personally knew Nin who died in 1977? Raab reveals that Nin taught her the intrinsic value of the written word; intrinsic, not as so many pennies a page or as literary acclaim, but as one's own words delivering comfort in the impassive night, one's own phrases illuminating and clarifying the days ahead. Raab also tells us that Anaïs Nin's *Diaries* taught her the importance of having love in one's life, and, indeed these are poems about having love: for parent, grandparent, husband, lover, and for life itself, for the physical thrill of existence.

While Raab understands the essence of Anaïs Nin's work, she expresses it in a voice all her own. Nin's voice overflowed in expansive prose, while each of Raab's poems is a pinprick of precision, a deceptively casual, all-American haiku. Derived from her journals, Raab's poems record the everyday delights that a diarist notices: composted coffee grinds and grapefruit rinds re-appearing on the table as a juicy tomato, putting her feet into duck slippers to take the dog out in the morning, seeing her grandpa's soft hands years later on a stranger. Like Nin, Raab finds her material in the nooks and corners unique to woman's experience: kissing her first boyfriend at Woodstock and their braces locking, mature, finely tuned erotic encounters, the cut of breast cancer, the slap of hot flashes, and the humor of receiving a disappointing salon massage at the hands of an Italian masseur.

Anaïs in her *Diary* assembled a lengthy woman's bildungsroman from such deeply received moments, each as a discrete journal entry. In worthy tribute, Raab has created a minimalist memoir, a chronology of her heightened moments, each crafted into a perfectly focused poem.

Tristine Rainer
Author of *The New Diary* and *Your Life as Story*

Dear Anaïs:

Ever since discovering your journals nearly ten years ago, I have kept them stacked on my bedside table. Although I've read the collection from beginning to end, lately I've found myself randomly flipping through to read some of your very compelling passages. Your words have inspired my own, and for years, whenever I have been stuck or my pen negotiated its flow, I've turned to your diaries for inspiration.

While studying your history, I learned that there were parallels in our lives. My grandmother and mentor, Regina Klein, was also born in 1903, and, like you, she was a diarist. Your death in 1977 was only months before my marriage to the love of my life, Simon.

Some time ago, I wrote a letter to your brother, Joaquin, but much to my chagrin, he never wrote back. I looked for any, albeit minute, connection to your spirit and some way of showing my appreciation for your presence in my life.

This year I was delighted to have been invited to an event at The Los Angeles Hammer Museum to what would have been your 105th birthday celebration. This was one of the highlights of my adult life. Presentations were given by some of your dearest friends—Tristine Rainer, Deena Metzger, Bebe Barron, and Eric Lloyd Wright. I wish you could have been there as they shared anecdotes from encounters with you, as well as some of your written passages. It was interesting to hear Tristine say how you taught her to dig deeper with her writing, something you also taught me just by the nature of reading your work.

I also liked your entries about the house Eric built for you and Rupert. One of everyone's fascinating revelations was how you had two husbands at the same time—one in Los Angeles and one in New York—and how you spent six weeks with one and then the other. Apparently, some of your friends knew about your lifestyle, but it wasn't revealed openly until after your death. Everyone spoke of you with such high regard, how you loved parties and helping people, and how you were so sensitive to other people's needs, and to those in your circle you were the best possible friend.

This new connection to you makes me feel even closer, and it seems even more poignant that I dedicate this book of poems to you this year. My poetry was born in my journal and tells the story of my life. The poems were all written from my heart and fluctuate from a deep place of pain to a high state of joy.

You've taught me the intrinsic value of the written word, how to dig deeper into my emotional truth, and the importance of having love in my life. And for all these gifts, I thank you.

With love,
Diana
Santa Barbara, CA
August 2008

Dedicated to

Anaïs Nin

February 21, 1903 – January 14, 1977

Each Winter Sunday

Klein's

An elevated train screeched to a halt
as I stood knee-high at Grandpa's register.
Brooklyn, 1961. Smell of gasoline.
Squeaky doors opening. The train's whistle

in the distance echoing louder until
it drowned our voices.
It stops. The doors open and as quickly
as it arrived, it disappears out of view

onward to the next station, until the next
arrives from the opposite direction.
People of every shape and color unload,
balanced by shopping bags and landing

onto the littered street below. This
pattern continues all day long
until nighttime when we mount

the same train back to our quiet
neighborhood in Queens where the loudest
sound you'll hear is a cat crying in the
dead of a hot summer night.

Jones Beach

Each Sunday morning
of my childhood, I looked
forward to rising at seven

before other vehicles
were loaded with beach toys
and coolers, as my mother

and grandmother crammed
our used Valiant with bottled water,
sandwiches on stale pumpernickel bread

smeared with cream cheese and one slab
of bologna, wrapped in wax paper
because Mom was an environmentalist

and tin foil was not biodegradable.
Mother put them in a frayed woven
picnic basket beside a bag of carrots,

box of chocolate chip cookies
and unwashed Macintosh apples.
Once after getting home we read

the small print on the box and learned
that those cookies were appetite
suppressants. I wish I had a handful

of them now, as I glance down
and notice the extra tire traveling
with me through my menopause.

Something else to thank my mother for.

Rockefeller

Each winter Sunday, instead
of working in the store,
my father went to our garage

and fetched the black bag
from the rack, holding his
figure skates and drove

to the city to teach skating
at Rockefeller Center beneath
the nine-ton Christmas tree.

On a good day, he taught five
or six stars, like Paul Newman,
who gave him autographed photos

which decorated our basement walls,
until Mom had a clean-up day and tossed
all his memories into the Goodwill box.

Now Dad's memories hang
on the walls of people we never met,
and others who have no clue.

Figure Skating

From ages six to twelve
I took a bus from school
to Mom's office where she

worked as a doctor's assistant,
around the corner from the skating rink
where I did figure eights and spins

three times a week. I quit lessons
after losing too many competitions
and discovering boys were more fun.

My mom still figured the hobby
would bring Dad and me closer,
After my lessons, Mom and I

stopped at the Starlight diner
where the waiter behind the counter
already knew I wanted spaghetti

and meatballs with lots of sauce,
but still came over on his roller skates,
which sometimes lost a wheel because

he did too many tricks. Once he told me
roller skating was safer than figure skating.
I learned early not to argue with a man.

The Stable

Each Sunday my mother's stable
was the church I attended
holding an apple and carrot

for Lucknow Guy, the male
in her life, standing eighteen
hands high awaiting our predictable

weekly visit. They performed their rituals,
him lifting his front leg towards her,
she placing the apple into his mouth

and petting his chestnut mane.
They stopped to momentarily stare
into one another's eyes until he

turned back to chomp on
his apple. She gathered his reins,
and ushered him to the corral

as my sneezes trailed behind,
in spite of the forced immunity
jammed into my upper right arm

two days each week for the second
five years of my life.
I hate how horses make me feel.

Composted

On the speckled Formica counter
of my childhood home, a yellow

strainer sat in the corner
under the window collecting

remnants of organics—coffee grains,
orange peels, apple cores, grapefruit rinds.

Every Monday my mother dumped
them onto the pile in the back right

corner of the yard, forgotten for months
until the soil was born and then tossed

into the spring's new tomato bed, whose fruit
the following summer made its way

back onto the kitchen counter,
in a new form—round, red and juicy.

Weekly Lottery

Giving in to his obsessions
was one thing my father did
almost every day of his life
for the fifty years which
he lived after The Holocaust
which robbed him of his parents
and baby brother Josh, putting
him and his brother in Dachau's
kitchen, slicing potatoes and
saving friends from starvation
as the Nazis dined off Rosenthal
plates confiscated from Jews
tossed into frigid barracks and
stripped of everything ever
important to them.

Dad's first treat, after arriving
in the United States with his brother Bob,
was using his factory paycheck for
a weekly lottery ticket, awaiting
the easy windfall, a sham of
good fortune, as if winning
the lottery was a ticket for a
new freedom boat. His
bliss stretched to winning five
tickets, five more scratches of
horizontal square boxes with
the same 1945 nickel which
he always carried in his pocket
for good luck, maybe not
enough cents to keep the
inveterate smoker alive past 70.

Love Chains

During the yearnings
of my youth, I dream
of the multi-colored love chains

crafted for boyfriends
from gum wrappers ripped in half,
folded four times and woven together

to their height, and ceremoniously
presented as a souvenir of our love,
until dentists shouted that too much gum

rotted our teeth. The sugarless kind
had boring wrappers. In return, the guys
gave us silver bracelets engraved

with their names, and we swore
not to lose them, as our fragile
adolescent wrists were weighed

down with the chain of silver, stamping
us for taken, as if the hunk of metal could
ever stop young wandering eyes.

Those Times

I swallowed my first dose of LSD the day my grandfather
fell to the floor from a heart attack. The drug eased
me into a glossy world devoid of pain.

Rebellion flavored my world, peace sign pins and beads
strung around my neck. I read Ayn Rand and Hermann Hesse
by day, and Jackie Collins by night.

My cut-off jeans angered my father who asked if I'd
been hired as a street cleaner. Long bangs flickered
while blinking, highlighting the Twiggy lines beneath.

The headshop of my neighborhood—Nirvana,
waited with beaded doors and jasmine incense,
cabinets of pipes and hippie jewelry and posters
of rock stars, illuminated by black lights.

I still ate TV dinners in my room. Gray mashed potatoes,
sweet corn and stewed peaches combined in the compartments
of an aluminum tray. For a treat, Horn and Hardart sat around
the corner where slices of runny cherry pie rotated in their cabinet.

I touched Clapton's elbow through a chain-link
fence and jumped so high, hitting the overhang above.

Then there was my drive to Woodstock, being squashed in a crowd,
the smell of marijuana and kissing my first boyfriend
before our braces linked while wearing his silver ID bracelet
and Sergeant Pepper jacket. People swore I looked like
Elizabeth Taylor then. I never fathomed it, while glancing
in the mirror at my acne-stricken face, like my daughter's now.

Nirvana Dreams

Stepping through its beaded door
was like walking into a time cloud.

Whiffs of marijuana and hashish pipes
lined up by color in the cabinet
to the right, behind which stood
a hippie and his girl.

With beads and long hair
they lived in the VW van
parked in the rear of the store.

Their fenders splattered with colorful
peace signs like the psychedelic posters
on their store's walls glowing
under the corner black light.

Nirvana—a safe haven, offering
a calm transcending my fifteen-year-old psyche.

The freedom to wander through
without shoes or purchase.

The place exuded the potent energy
of my love generation.

I wish there was a store like it here
in my neighborhood now.

I'll settle for the natural health
food store, which offers the same sort of claim.

No One Else Was Home

To Dettner (My Grandmother)

You took your life in the house where

we lived together forty years ago.
I was ten and you sixty.

Your ashen face and blonde bob
disheveled upon white sheets

on the stretcher held by paramedics
lightly grasping each end, and tiptoeing

down the creaking wooden stairs
you walked up the night before.

But now your body descended to the ambulance
and sirens swarmed like vultures

around the place I once called home.
I wonder why you left in such a way,

as the depression gnawed
at your gentle heart, which cared for me

since my very first push into the world.
I've learned from you

never to give up, but to find
a passion and thank you.

I did.
I live to write

so I shall never die.

Revisited

The moment the helicopter crashed
in the field behind my house, my heart
skipped a beat and I couldn't help
but think of my grandfather whose aorta
busted at the age of eighty-three
while on his morning stroll
around our rather small block,
me back then, barely thirty and nearly
a grandparent myself. No one
was hurt, but the wings got
smashed up, and Grandpa died
before he hit the pavement.

Even this many years later,
I still wonder what his face
looked like in the pine coffin
Mother picked because she was cheap
and no one else was home.

To My Father

You had this radiant smile
and handshake to fracture a bone
and a giving heart
never with bad intention,
risked tossing the shirt
off your back to beggars on the street.

As a child I sat on the borders of
Rockefeller Center as you taught
Paul Newman to skate each Sunday
morning in the place where they called
you Mr. Mark because they couldn't
pronounce your long European last name.

We'd return home for steak and
whipped potatoes and then
vanilla pudding, your favorite meal
before your bedtime snack of
pumpernickel bread with a smear
of cream cheese.

In the morning I eyed you sitting
in the corner diner
as you flattered waitresses
and made them giggle with your charm,
as they poured you steamy coffee
in the same seat every morning,
where all you regulars arrived
promptly before six a.m.

After two decades since your passing,
I miss you more than ever and relish
every moment in which your

spirit encircles me. I still talk to you
each day, you the only person who
always loved me no matter what.

I shall be forever warmed by you.

Grandfather's Hands

Tonight I noticed his hands,
a little wrinkled, with fine hair
and square-shaped nails, like the ones

my manicurist always pushes
on me. I stopped short to stare at a displaced
familiarity and then realized his hands
were those of my beloved grandfather

who died twenty-five years earlier, under
the medical student's scalpel, side by side
a troop of doctors rummaging around
his aorta trying to arrest the bleeding

which eventually took Grandpa from me.
I hadn't seen those hands in all that time
or maybe longer because I lived too far away
to hold them on his death bed,

but their softness and lines remain engraved in
my fading memory with images of moments
from my childhood when we held hands
walking the streets of Paris each year

when he took me to visit his sister
and how he taught me to people
watch in the cafés, and how to use a journal.
This friend's hands bring back Grandpa's spirit,

nestled in the disbelief that someone
from my childhood neighborhood,
just around the corner from the house
where Grandpa read the paper on the porch,
might have hands like his.

My Navigator

Dedicated to Aunt Lilly

From the moment we met
I loved you, right there
in your country house on a remote lake,
Hungarian cheese spread smeared
on Swedish crackers, chicken paprika
draped over a mound of mashed potatoes,
that long French Canadian wood table,
delightful culinary aromas from your kitchen,
lively paintings and portraits enveloping your walls,
books piled on your bedside table —

Oh how I miss the warmth of your home,
nestled in your easy laugh and zest for life—

I knew I wanted to grow old like you,
proud shoulders pulled back,
despite years in concentration camp
and the loss of two adoring husbands.

I shall forever be impressed
by your sense of humor, how you called
my husband the glue doctor after he
developed a prosthetic cement; your fine
attire as a clothing designer, your positive tint
to life's idiosyncrasies, and yearning
for learning and travel.

I sit here with the memory
of your accented voice and how you
said you had to go to your room to
'brush your tits,' and how each time
we looked into one another's eyes

we had a connection which transcended
any words I could blend on these lines.

You've helped me navigate through every
stage of this woman's life and shown me
how to survive until the day I am pulled by
whatever chooses to take me.

I Must Have Been Chinese in a Past Life

Like the Chinese I have this perpetual
habit of asking people their vital numbers—
birthday, phone number and address,
as if the answers provide the window
into their soul and personality, or maybe
it's just that number patterns offer me
a sort of internal solace.

They say the number eight
is the most fortuitous of numbers,
to mathematicians, a composite
and power of two, and for skaters like me,
constitutes the geometric shape
of compulsory figures drawn to three
times one's height, like at the rink

I frequented as a kid five times a week
for skating lessons with Vera, the instructor
with the leather strap terrorizing me
into making the most perfect eight of all,
even better than the ones in my hand
of cards Grandma dealt during
our nightly game of Crazy Eights.

It's no wonder that today when buying
shiny silver bangles, I counted not seven
or nine, but eight, the number which pledges
to bring good luck and power and maybe
one of those "After Eight" chocolates
which Mom bought me for my birthday
the year before she died.

Mother's Neighborhood

When the sun rises in my mother's
quiet town, you can hear
car engines start, children crying
about going to school while climbing

into the buses zooming up
these suburban streets,
but my mother, a widow
for fifteen years, sees only

her microcosm—her cat, Lilly
at the foot of her bed, the cyclamens
on the kitchen table awaiting
her weekly waterings, the refrigerator

with four eggs, a container
of sour milk and some carrots
for her horse. It's Monday
and she tosses her laundry into

a plastic bag, flings it into the trunk
of her brown Honda and heads
to the local laundromat
where the other lonely locals

hang out awaiting the end
of their spin cycles as they convene
on splintered benches pressed
to the frigid outside window,

sharing neighborly gossip
and puffing on menthol cigarettes,
glancing left to the poorer
section of town, and right

to where the rich folk live.
Mom isn't quite sure
on which side of the tracks she belongs.
In her mothball closet

she hides a fur coat from Grandma,
in its pocket a diamond ring never worn.
In the basement washing machine
she stashes emergency funds,
and family heirlooms in unmarked boxes.
Because of Mother's bunions
she wears orthodic sneakers with long skirts,
and would much rather be seen

with the less fortunate, they don't stare at her garb,
they just talk behind her back and wonder.

Poetry As Bird

Sketch of a Writer's Studio

Empty coffee-imbued mugs,
remnants of tea leaves
in blue Chinese tea pots,

a dimly lit purple lamp,
stacks of crinkled purple file folders
busting with shreds of wisdom,

dusty antique typewriters interspersed
with writing manuals and memoirs
once alphabetical, photos of my loved ones,

both here and gone, faded artistry of daughters
now on their own, a reading chair
beside a purple orchid crowded by

a crooked pile of books laden with stickers
on their best pages, purple pens
and yellow highlighters

clinging as bookmarks, pads of notes,
boxes of dated journals,
tins of obsolete manuscripts

flipped open for ideas,
scented creativity candles,
a sunburst mirror with an image

of the back of a computer screen,
paned doors facing the outside
water fountain shared with hummingbirds

and rabbits nibbling at fallen rose petals.
An Oriental end table harbors
a pen collection beside a floor heater

to dry the tears which pour from me
as this gel pen negotiates its flow.

There's a Story in Everything

Wherever you turn—above your head,
behind your back, under your ass,
you'll find a story.

It might be of the old lady exercising
her little white dog or the young
skateboarder skipping curbs or the bus

driver who's driven fifteen straight hours
or the server whose tips are less than
her paycheck or the computer fix it guy

who walks up 2033 Sixth Street to visit
the same household of nerds or the bartender
who holds everyone's secrets or the ice cream

man who lives to see kids dashing towards
his truck or the jewelry maker scouting
the perfect diamond or the mayor of any

small town inventing ways to make people
stop littering or the gardener who always runs
out of gas or the TV repairman suggesting

to replace the television or the iPod which the mom
can't get working or the hairstylist who had a fight
with her lover and can't lend a good hair day

or the guitarist who keeps snapping his strings
or the drummer who splits his sticks or the lawyer
who loses the case or the father who wants a girl

but neglects to remember the full moon or the race car
driver who took the bend too wide and never
saw his first grandchild born the very next day.

Poetry As Bird

Poems transport us
        across
the ether and layers
of our quilted skies
to unknown
        horizons
and glistening galaxies
displaying emblems
of bliss propelled by
         wings
of time, and a tomorrow
which might never be.
Fly with me to the place

where nothing matters
but today's reveries which
        whisper
words of infinite possibility.

On Demand

When you asked me
to write you a poem
that day we took a walk
behind your house

moments after making
crazy love in the hammock
hanging from your mammoth oak tree
under the stars, clothes strewn

about the freshly cut grass
where rabbits made babies
and shuttles dropped
their solid rocket boosters,

I told you that I couldn't
do anything on demand,
not even tell you what a
great lover you were.

Never on demand.

You should also know
I told my poetry mentor
the same. I do things when I want to,
not when told, except of course

if you asked me with your seductive voice

to make love in that hammock again,
hanging upside down like the sloth
we spotted at the zoo today,
everything in slow motion,

and under the vibrant stars
holding a new poem in my head
as we rocked in the hammock
moments after our long walk
and fervent love-making.

Tides of Wonder

Sometimes when I sit
alone before the ocean,
crocheted mittens
peeking through warm
wrappings of winter wools
sandwiched between
daily responsibilities,
my mind stretches
across extrasolar horizons,

sprinkled with flecks of blue skies,
as my dog's ears
perk to my internal whispers
for a hopeful tomorrow.

We sit nestled beside splintered
driftwood of yesterday,
stretching ten birds wing span

and dream of spreading
our own wings, as poets
try to decipher which
word to pluck

from their succulent buckets
to sprinkle into a medley which
one day in their dreams
or in some reality
will blossom into famous verse.

Sheets

To Write a Poem

slip into your negligee,
lean your face toward the sheets

smell the intimacy,
anticipate the words,

caress and grasp
the bliss of the moment

as adjectives whet your appetite
and verbs propel you forward.

Feel the juices flow as you dip
into whispers and tastes of euphoria

which pour into the lyrics of your new life
as the warmth of two bodies unites.

I Arrive Early

Dedicated to Sharon Olds

I arrive early in this room
because I want to soak up
your energy and every drop
of your spirit. I want my notebook,
my scarf, my pants, my shirt,
my socks, to be saturated with your words.

I am happy to be here.

If you proclaim that everything
happens for a reason, then surely
mine is that poetry is my calling now
and I need to be engulfed by your karma
as only you can release the poet in me
and set me free.

Trust me. I wear purple.

Dampened Creativity

Once I took an anti-depressant
but never again, thank you.

The little pill locked up my writing voice
where creating a sentence became a task

of impossible extraction. Unlike before
as lyrics were my panacea when falling

into life's darkest alleys like learning
I had breast cancer at forty-seven.

So I flushed those little yellow pills
down the toilet and found my journal

in the desk drawer, and let
my fountain pen slide across its pages.

This simple gesture cured me then
and will forever shelter me from

demons which want to continuously
slash my throat and pull away my joy.

Those Fine Strings

Laws of Attraction

In seventh grade
my physics teacher
took us on his sailboat.
He was a tall blue-eyed,
gray-haired guy
with a smile that
could power his vessel.

Dr. Cotton's lightness of being
pulled me in like the inertia
he professed. It's no wonder
that twenty years later I fell
for another physicist who
taught me that life
is all about energy.

Crossword

He and I
our first date
over a crossword puzzle,

couldn't stop giggling
while struggling on a clue
I thought belly-like sounds;

he thought bell-like sounds.
He was right, as he's been
for the past thirty years, like the day

he said I should write poetry—
it would be healthy, like a mother
saying the same of spinach. I abhorred

Chaucer in grade school, memorizing
words never understood, but now words
are my game and sustenance.

I reminisce about family Scrabble games,
fighting for the right place on the squares
giving the most points—Zip, Zoo, Zed

and then for never-heard-of words
snuck from the dictionary
he gave me for our first anniversary.

Your Voice

The sound of your voice
is like honey in my morning coffee

sunlight extending across the Pacific,
a vestal snowfall on a crisp Saturday,

the peeking through of the first spring flower,
smell of a newborn baby, to an acceptance letter,

love sounds in the night, the wagging of my puppy's
tail, piping hot maple syrup on pancakes,

cracking open your newly released book,
the look of a rushing waterfall, the regal

mountains, the snapping of an open fire,
gooey marshmallows on fraying sticks,

the warmth of your arms which promised
to hold me all century long, until we see

the next turn of the zodiac when we learn
we were born and will die under the same star.

You Always Want to Have Breakfast

You always want to meet
on that quiet street, inside the diner
with the flickering neon sign

where you wait in the booth
with the ripped red vinyl seat,
just past the rotating bar stools,
near the juke box which never works,

sipping your day's first cup
of brown brew, as I strut
through the revolving door

flashing the red heels you ask
me to wear because you say
they make my calves flex

the way you like them,
muscles I earned after years of
figure skating each day
after school at the rink

near your house, until
I discovered boys like you
were more fun than doing figures.

Venus Fly Trap

Each night in my dreams
your claw-like arms sit wide open
flickering, trying to attract me
into your essence.

I nudge closer to you.

Before my touch, you withdraw
and again I'm tricked by you.
Like one hundred nights before,
I'm struck by your charm,

your long lashes and dimples,
each time more intense, until I decide
to fight my desire and drift away.
And again you cast your spell on me,

I turn around and reach for you—
but you're gone. I stand up
and call your name,
and suddenly your spirit lands

on my bedside table. I waste no time.
I approach you and tell you that I surrender.

I am yours.

The Mirror and Your Face

I look in the mirror and see your face
looking back at me
wondering what happened
to the good times we spent
evaporated like the steam
of my kettle
getting ready to pour
my morning coffee
which lifts my head up
from the hole where it's buried
because you left me.

Do you also see my face
in your mirror
smiling and wondering
where you went on
that cold day
when you said good-bye
because you couldn't take
the stress of loving me deeply
without rest from
morning until night.

The day we went for the walk
in the park I glanced hard
at my face in my pocket mirror.
We fed the ducks, sat in the grass,
necked and rolled down the hill,
you on top first then me,
we stopped only at water's edge
as an alligator peeked his eyes
from the murky water, and
reached for your toe. I grabbed
my mirror, but it was too late,
you were gone.

The Visitation

It's been a long day
in this foreign city

and I return to my hotel room
toss off my red sandals and fling

their matching purse on the bed
where you lay the night before.

I unravel my mind and methodically
remove my clothes and plop my tired body

on the sofa to stare at the bed where
you brought the woman out in me,

long after my precipitous mid-life blues.
I have no idea if your visit was a dream

or a strike of desired reality and I don't
suppose you'll ever confess as I stare

into your glassy eyes during our
morning coffee, and watch them turn

cold like the icicle suspended from the roof
before you grab its point and jam

it into my mouth, for the last time before
you walk out the door back to her.

The Blues

You may think
I like the music
or the rhythm of the band,
but what I speak of
is the sadness which engulfs
my spirit in this gloomy isolation
of unexplainable origins.

A dizzying sense of blackness
churns about me. I see
no wonders created here.
My tears swell like the foam
of the cappuccino which opens
my eyelids each morning
when I really don't want
to face another day of loneliness.

I hunt for a place to turn, but am blinded
by doors slamming around my ventricles
and as my heart is squeezed like a girdle
to useless hips. I am blinded
by my pain and realize that it's time
to die to the sounds of palpitating whispers.

I Am Your Slave

I am pulled into your energy
I am yanked into all your good
I borrow your breaths

as I search for my last one
wondering what I was thinking
when you reached for me and I

said okay before pulling back
into my cocoon which wrapped
its protective strings around me.

So many days later, you came back,
pulled those fine strings to unravel
my world watching me spin in circles

to release myself from your grasp.
I am your slave and there's no other way
of looking at this predicament I am in.

Turning Fifty in an Italian Village

So I made the leap and requested
a massage in the Italian salon

fantasizing about how his hands
would knead my tired soul and body

with their strength and finesse,
only to learn that the weakling artist

knew not how to touch the female body,
but only how to sculpt it, as his

sexy grandeur turned on my
lymphatic tap to get the juices flowing,

while moving his hands up and down
my anatomy missing all the muscles,

and treating them as clay.
So what I have done is pay

for his pleasure, because all I feel
is more tense than before I lay

down on his sculpting table.
Thanks, for nothing, Romeo.

Dear Stranger

Your eyes spoke
a language I understood,

the only rope stretching
between us, everything else

separated by a universe
and droves of years.

Your tall, dark and handsome
youth wanted me in a big way

and a bigger way when I sat alone
as my husband meandered into the w.c.
and you gave me a moment of you.

I pushed to ignore the short-lived
intensity of our magnetic attraction

because in the end it wouldn't matter,
but as a woman entering her sixth decade

your desire ripped me from my complacency,
until there in the Naples airport you put on your

sunglasses and wheeled your suitcase out
from baggage claim, turned around

and slid them to the tip of your nose,
licked your lips from side to side,

smiled and walked outside, thrusting into your
world and sending me back into mine.

behind her back

I just met you
and want you,
yet you're so young

    so fragile,

    so curious

    so nice

    so desirable

    so tender

    so unsure

of yourself and me
of us
of the other blonde
at your side,
and of the drink
and snack we nibbled
behind her back.

Caesarean Words

The words you write
cut me open
like a caesarean birth,
and lance a hole
in my wounded world
as I know to be good,
but now, after we made
love, you decided
to stay much longer
than the scars
from my babies
and the snow
which melted
on yesterday's grass.

A Dictionary of Secret Lovers

aflutter: what her heart felt when she saw him step onto the sand

capricious: as the sister of unpredictable, she knew this to be part of the enticement

elegy: the reflective story she wrote after their four-hour romantic encounter

ennui: how she felt when she was with her last lover

ephemeral: how she summed up the nature of their rendezvous

fantasize: what she did when she couldn't be with him

faux pas: what he made when he'd asked if she had liposuction

fervent: how she felt once they climbed into bed together and snuggled under the heated blanket

fortuitous: the nature of their chance encounter on a nude beach on the day where no one else showed up

lascivious: the way she described his lust; a praying mantis closing in on a new found bug

maxim: the general truth was that it was all a dream

muse: his effect on her creativity whenever his eyes slipped under her skin

nexus: the center of their orgasmic moment seemed to last for an eternity

nidget: what she called the person who said they'd be sexually incompatible nugget: the lump of firm gold found in his pants

orchid: the beautiful showy flower which in Greek describes his testicle

purple: the psychic color uniting their spirits

rhetoric: his word choice at the right moment sending her into an orgasmic frenzy

serendipitous: their midnight encounter which was meant to be

tenacious: the determination of two kindred spirits sharing multi-orgasmic moments

sticky wicket: a situation where there is no way out—they could have been caught in the act

vehement: how they felt when the knock on the door interrupted their evening's pinnacle

wanderlust: having the need to escape extremely quickly

Surrender

Hot Flashed Mama

Three kids later
umpteen years of marriage
closets stacked with baby photos

boxes of tight pre-pubescent clothes,
molded dolls, kindergarten drawings,
and unsent letters, all responsible

for days spent at the hairdresser
covering up a past, multiple Mondays
of smashed alarm clocks, visits

to bookstores and doctors for
lifelines of holistic hope, burrowed
in the darkness of far flung blankets.

In the night—dry vaginas, mood dips,
migraine-filled cerebellums, surprising

drips from past lives, forgetful moments,
cravings for departures criss-crossed
with the bliss of freedom and fear of loneliness.

All in the name of womanhood.

I surrender.

Prisms of My Mind

You might glance at me
and never imagine

certain things about me
like how at night I bite my cuticles

and eat dark chocolate
in my walk-in closet

and collect unusual shoes
and antique typewriters.

You might also not notice
the many facets of my blues,

hidden in the mirrors
of my mind, barely seen

on the creases of my face
but definitely in my living space

braided into my ruminations
about the universe during

moments when all I can do
is create dark poems

which hopefully one day
will evaporate into happy tears,

as I drip calming chemicals under
my shrived middle-aged menopausal tongue.

A Woman's Life

Kicking
Wiggling
Sucking
Pushing
Nursing
Sleeping
Eating
Growing
Crawling
Sitting
Walking
Counting
Reading
Writing
Biking
Dancing
Flirting
Necking
Loving
Cramping
Rebelling
Driving
Exercising
Studying
Working
Marrying
Nurturing
Obsessing
Separating
Crying
Dieting
Menopausing
Wrinkling

Grouching
Forgetting
Slouching
Dying.

Butterfly Dreams

Dedicated to S.R.

I am a butterfly
drawn into the vapors
of your worship
on the ethers of my
horizons swerving on
the hills and waves,
caressing my world.
I plead for wellness and love
to forever surround my cocoon.

Wanting

I
Rainbow

The rain trickles
down my paned window
as I stand up to hunt the sky
for the stripes of my childhood.
The more I want to touch
that rainbow, the more it drifts away.

II
Persuasion

When you wonder about
what you want anew
try persuading yourself
and the answer will come to you.

III
Wishing Well

Yesterday I released a penny
in that deepest tunnel
of darkness, crossing my fingers
and begging for wellness.

Message to My Family

The day after I die
and hours after my ashes cool,
find a purple urn with a window.

Purple nurtures my spiritual strength
and windows keep me alive. Remember
I'm claustrophobic and the thought

of being stuck inside a box frightens me,
since I must indulge in my favorite hobby
of people-watching, which drives me

to my journal where I find joy and solace.
Remember writers need time alone—
and once a day my window should be closed,

just once a day after I die.

Massage Therapist

I remove my clothes and offer him
my nudeness, but am skeptical
that like many others in his profession,

his touch will be too light and miss
the muscles beneath. I live in hope
this time will be different and my old aches,

from the accident years before,
will be soothed by his touch.
He asks if I want deep tissue.

I nod and admit it takes a lot
to hurt me. In broken English
he tells me he will please me

and I'll leave feeling satisfied.
While hanging my robe on the hook
behind the door, I ponder his words

and then all I remember are his whispers
saying it was nice meeting me
and that I should get up slowly.

I thank him. He leaves the room
and I try standing, but my dizziness
captures my feet and I realize

I'd much rather have the stress
of broken bones than the kind
that messes up my mind.

Park Avenue

Why is it that men
always watch me park
as if they want to run over
and say 'lady look what you did'
thinking I'd crash, but never have.
My dad taught me to park
tightly in New York
and I'm good, but those guys
want to say 'just like a woman driver.'
Then I yell out 'damn it don't stare'
you asshole, you get me nervous,
do something productive with your time,
plus why are you sitting on the park benches
facing the street in front of my office
as your older wives shop in the stores
buying nothing, yet trying on things
which rarely fit like years ago.
They are my age now and looking back
at the styles and memories
which are now history
but like fire hydrants
pop up again randomly
when we least expect it.

Road Desperation

Tenth day on the road
and you love Starbucks
so early in the day, you schlep
across Iowa City to find a coffee,
then return to your hotel room,
and remove the lid. The drink is now
four inches from the cup's top. Foam
which was once warm, rests on the bottom
and you wish you had a longer tongue
but since you don't, you search for anything
that can reach the bottom of your Grande.
You frantically rummage through your suitcase,
then the bathroom and finally into your toiletry
bag, then you glance over to the sink and there's
the handle of your toothbrush, the perfect scoop.
You pray no one will see your cappuccino meeting
your toothbrush. You realize, for the first time,
that Colgate is nothing like sugar, especially
sitting on the end of a toothbrush.

How We Worry

Writers worry about stories
salesmen worry about selling
bus drivers worry about stopping
kids worry about homework
maids worry about dust

musicians worry about tunes
dogs worry about their owner's whereabouts
cats worry about the next bowl of milk
birds worry about nests
grandmas worry about grandchildren

growers worry about rain
taxi drivers worry about tips
pilots worry about the weather
nurses worry about cardiac arrests
doctors worry about getting sued
stewardesses worry about rages

students worry about exams
lawyers worry about winning the case
alcoholics worry about whiskey
booksellers worry about best sellers

boutique owners worry about styles
filmmakers worry about edits
engineers worry about measurements
chefs worry about scorching
journalists worry about deadlines

joggers worry about injuries
programmers worry about viruses
bank tellers worry about cash flow

wine makers worry about berries
teachers worry about attendance

and I worry about what will happen
to my heart when you decide to leave.

Early Morning Tossings

Like the shakes brought on
by earthquakes, the flash

of middle age flung me
from my bed at two a.m.,

covers tossed
to the wooden floor,
my Japanese fan

flung open and gulps
of ice water wet
the furnace inside me

and then the touch
of my beloved—the
hand squeeze

to get me over
one more hurdle
facing the womanhood

I couldn't wait to reach,
and now
can't wait to finish.

Can I Buy Time?

If I needed to, could I buy time, by splitting my bankbook open, selling heirloom jewels, the tiled roof over my head or the floral garden where my dog roams?

And what is buying time? Is it a slowing down and valuing what we have? Or is it a focusing on now, living in the moment without looking forward or backward?

How is it that I stand still and my life flashes before me. Does this mean I've bought time? If yes, then it surely wasn't enough.

The Real Solace

Rituals

We share everything,
except of course, my love
and the chocolate bar
hidden in my bedside drawer.
He stretches up to the side
of my bed to say good morning,

before I slide into my duck slippers
that he nibbles on my way to the bathroom.
Together we walk to the balcony and down the stairs
to the garden so he can do his business.

He jolts at the slightest rustling in the bush,
or bird chirping, ears sharp like
the razor my love uses each morning.
We run back inside, me to push the button
for my morning espresso, and for the treat

he knows waits in the cabinet beneath
the kitchen sink beside his dog food.
He scrutinizes every movement of mine.
When I go to the windowsill where

his leash awaits, he wags his tail
and stares up at me with an equal amount
of adoration and anticipation. Then
he turns upside down and I rub
his tummy and say *let's go.*

Windows

As a little girl I hated looking out windows after sunset. The fear
began one night at the age of eight while I walked down the creaky
wooden stairs of my childhood home for a bedtime snack of milk and
cookies. I turned the corner to face our yard and my eyes were drawn
to a moving figure in the same place where so many years before sat
my inflatable baby pool with ducks painted on its bottom. The creep
wore a woolen mask slipped over his face leaving dots for his onyx
eyes. Like a jellybean, he jumped from side to side and signaled me
to come to him. Petrified, I scurried back up the stairs, getting railing
burn as I ran, and finally landing in the arms of my doll, sprawled
across my bed. I pulled her towards me holding on tight as if she
could save me from myself. The truth is, she was the only one I ever
trusted.

My Imaginary World

People drip with stories
and linger in bookstores and cafés
slurping foamy cappuccinos
and nibbling on chocolate cake
or crème caramel, flipping through
their latest writings while
jotting down thoughts
on the notebooks of their minds.

In my imaginary world
people have antennas
to feel what others feel
to be there when needed
and disappear when it's time.

In my imaginary world
poems don't need editing
and writers are never rejected.

In my imaginary world
friends last a lifetime,
keep in touch and nurture us
with memories and love.

In my imaginary world
kids have lots of kids
to swell the universe
with giggles and questions
dogs never die and lovers
understand that when
it's over, it's over.

In my imaginary world, we
become someone else, maybe
for a minute or an hour, or a day,

sometimes wishing for an eternity, but
the real solace comes in the
ephemeral quality of being different
for a short time. It is the change
of perspective that is welcome.

Illegal Feet

I sit here in a coffee house
slurping my iced Americano coffee,
my baseball cap obstructs the view
of what lies above everyone's knee

because all I want to know
is what shoes people wear.
Shoes tell it all, like the woman
over there in high heels,

wanting to be as tall as today's lover,
and tomorrow she'll wear flats
when out with her son. Then
there's the father who's

spending the weekend with his kid
sporting scuffed sneakers,
and the construction worker with tired
legs and steel-tipped boots.

In front of the line stands a man
illegally barefoot in this place with
coffee house rules plastered on all
six walls. What are the chances of
him drinking coffee with his feet?

A Longer Tongue Would Be Nice

Did you ever wish
you had a longer tongue

to scoop the foam from the bottom
of a cappuccino cup when

you've forgotten the spoon, or
to snag a piece of salad stuck

between your back teeth, or
to make the kids laugh
when you lick your nose
and cross your eyes, or

to use on your lover wherever, or
to lick the food off your cheek

when your hands are busy, or
when your ice cream drips faster
down the cone than the summer's heat

as it becomes sticky in your hands, and
napkins are nowhere to be found.

Emotional Baggage

When meeting someone for the first time
at a dinner party or writer's workshop
I glance at the color of their baggage.

I study their face—

the bags under their eyes,
lines around their mouths,
the crow's feet, pock marks,

and wrinkled necks, to see
how the years of their lives
have haunted them. The nature

and shape of their bags will lure
or repel me to want to get to know
them. I arrive home, look in the mirror

and observe my own worn lines and suitcases
and wonder what people may have been
muttering about me.

I'm stumped.

Luggage

From our past
we carry

rusty cars
holey socks
leaky pens
dull knives
war ballads
chipped teeth
patched jeans
fatigued flip flops
yellowing journals
caked soap dishes
crushed Coke cans
inverted umbrellas
bleeding hangnails
five-o'clock shadow
safety-pinned hems
expired prescriptions
extra holiday pounds
scratched sunglasses
dog-eared paperbacks
incomplete manuscripts
flat bristle toothbrushes
memory-depleted laptops
photographs without dates
TV dinners with uneaten vegetables
crumbled fortune cookie messages
and dreams of unknown futures.

Five Kitchen Poems

Cookies

Cut each day out
as if it were your last—
a good excuse to do
all of your favorite things.

Marinate

Use casseroles to repel evil
and enclose all the good,
left at room temperature
just the way you like it.

Ice Cubes

Put your stories
into the squares of an ice
cube tray and turn them
over, release as needed.

Sandwiches

Knead your whole wheat bread,
bake it, slice it and then smear
it with hot mustard to remind us
that pain is sharp, but then it passes.

Toast

Pour the champagne;
clap for the exuberances;
bow to the accomplishments;
and flush all the sorrows.

Let's All Eat Blueberries

What is it about
the missing sock
from the dryer
or pair of scissors
replaced every other day,
the vanished scotch tape
used to wrap yesterday's gift,
the brush which lay on
the vanity the night before,
the gas tank you just filled,
the wallet devoid of money,
the cookie jar once full,
the tapered nails gone astray,
the empty milk carton,
or the thirty years which
passed by leaving you with
blurred memories
of the wonder years.

Note: Researchers at the USDA Human Nutrition Center (HNRCA) have found that blueberries rank #1 in antioxidant activity when compared to 40 other fresh fruits and vegetables. Antioxidants help neutralize harmful by-products of metabolism called "free radicals" that can lead to cancer and other age related diseases, such as memory loss.

Appendix

Who is Anaïs Nin?

(February 21, 1903-January 14, 1977)

Anaïs Nin was a French-born author of Spanish, Cuban and Danish descent who became famous for her published diaries, which spanned more than sixty years of her life. She began writing in her diary when she was eleven years old. Her first diary began as a letter to her estranged father who left the family for another woman.

After her parents separated, her mother moved Anaïs and her two brothers, Thorvald Nin and Joaquin Nin-Culmell to New York City. While still a teenager, Anaïs abandoned formal schooling and began working as a model.

In March 1923, Nin married Hugh Parker Guiler, a banker and artist, and the couple moved to France where Anaïs began to pursue her interest in writing. Her first published work was a critical evaluation of D.H. Lawrence, *D.H. Lawrence: An Unprofessional Study*. She also explored the field of psychotherapy and studied under Otto Rank, a disciple of Sigmund Freud. In 1930, Nin and her husband moved back to New York City.

In 1955, while still married to Guiler, she married Rupert Pole, a forester and step-grandson of Frank Lloyd Wright. The wedding took place in Arizona and the couple then moved to California. Guilder was unaware of Nin's second marriage until after her death in 1977.

Ansïs Nin's diaries were considered literary nonfiction and were compelling for a number of reasons, particularly because she was quite intimate with a number of prominent authors, artists, and psychoanalysts. Her diaries portray these persons in an unusual depth of analysis and frankness of description.

About the Author

Diana M. Raab, is a poet, memoirist and essayist whose award-winning writings has appeared in national publications and anthologies.

Her most recent work includes a poetry chapbook, *My Muse Undresses Me* (Pudding House Publications, 2007) and a memoir, *Regina's Closet: Finding My Grandmother's Secret Journal* (Beaufort Books, 2007), recipient of the 2008 National Indie Award for Memoir. She's editor of *Writers and Their Notebooks* forthcoming by The University of South Carolina Press in 2009.

She teaches in the UCLA Extension Writers' Program, the Santa Barbara Writers' Conference and conducts journal-keeping workshops for writers and professionals around the country.

She lives in Santa Barbara, California with her husband and their Maltese poodle, Spunky. She has three grown children. Her website is http://www.dianaraab.com.

Acknowledgements

"To Dettner," A Treasury of American Poetry III; "Message to My Family," Chest; "A Longer Tongue Would Be Nice," Genie; "Luggage," Homestead Review; "The Stable," and "The Visitation," Litchfield Review; "Crossword," Lucidity; "Rockefeller," Main Channel Voices; "Revisited," Mystorylives.blogspot.com; "I Must Have Been Chinese in a Past Life," "Rituals," and Weekly Lottery," Poetry Superhighway; "Nirvana Dreams," Red River Review; "Revisited," Samizdada; "Sketch of a Writer's Studio," Oracle; "Park Avenue," Scribbles; "Love Chains," and "Your Voice," Snap Poetry Journal; "Those Times," Tapestries; "In My Imaginary World," The Binnacle; "Road Desperation," Writers Journal (Poetry Award – Honorable Mention).

Special thanks to Susan Bright for believing in this project and Maggie Lang for her technical and professional support. Also, special thanks to friends, colleagues and mentors who have inspired my poetry, including Molly Fisk, Molly Peacock, Denise Duhamel, Sharon Olds, David Starkey, Steve Reigns, Tristine Rainer, Suzannah Gilman, Darlyn Finch, Philip F. Deaver, Marcia Meier, Jean Harfenist, Melinda Palacio, Steve Beisner, Susan Pitcher and former poet laureate, Billy Collins, whose poetry reading in Louisville, Kentucky inspired me to write my first poem. He taught me how poetry could be both accessible and comforting.

In addition, I would like to thank my loving children, Rachel, Regine and Joshua who always want to read my poetry, and last but never least, my husband, Simon, for his support and unrelenting belief in my poetic voice.

Printed in the United States
130443LV00001B/247-345/P